OPENING A STORE?

FOLLOW THESE STEPS TO GET YOUR BUSINESS RUNNING SMOOTH

VIRGINIA HERNANDEZ

For information, contact Virginia Hernandez
1250 E Picacho Ave Apt#26
Las Cruces New Mexico 88005

Dedication

- To all the new business owners, in hope that this can make your new project a little more simple

How to use this workbook

With this workbook you can make sure you've done everything you need in your work day.

Check all that apply as you do them to stay organized

Daily
Steps

- ❑ Arrive 1 hour prior opening
- ❑ Deactivate alarm
- ❑ Make sure other employees arrive with you
- ❑ Turn on the lights on
- ❑ Make sure air conditioning/heating turned on
- ❑ Make sure merchandise is in order and dusted
- ❑ Check all money in cash register
- ❑ Open doors
- ❑ Have your best customer service attitude
- ❑ Make sure all employees have what they need for their duties
- ❑ Ask customers if they need help in anything
- ❑ Once a week take note of the inventory needed to restock merchandise
- ❑ Through out the day take notes of what people buy the most of the inventory purpose
- ❑ Make sure all customers have left the building
- ❑ Lock doors
- ❑ Count cash drawer and take out earnings, leave it ready for the next day
- ❑ Throw all trash
- ❑ Make sure employees all leave together and get to their car safe

Daily Notes

Daily
Steps

- ❏ Arrive 1 hour prior opening
- ❏ Deactivate alarm
- ❏ Make sure other employees arrive with you
- ❏ Turn on the lights on
- ❏ Make sure air conditioning/heating turned on
- ❏ Make sure merchandise is in order and dusted
- ❏ Check all money in cash register
- ❏ Open doors
- ❏ Have your best customer service attitude
- ❏ Make sure all employees have what they need for their duties
- ❏ Ask customers if they need help in anything
- ❏ Once a week take note of the inventory needed to restock merchandise
- ❏ Through out the day take notes of what people buy the most of the inventory purpose
- ❏ Make sure all customers have left the building
- ❏ Lock doors
- ❏ Count cash drawer and take out earnings, leave it ready for the next day
- ❏ Throw all trash
- ❏ Make sure employees all leave together and get to their car safe

Daily Notes

Daily
Steps

❑Arrive 1 hour prior opening

❑Deactivate alarm

❑Make sure other employees arrive with you

❑Turn on the lights on

❑Make sure air conditioning/heating turned on

❑Make sure merchandise is in order and dusted

❑Check all money in cash register

❑Open doors

❑Have your best customer service attitude

❑Make sure all employees have what they need for their duties

❑Ask customers if they need help in anything

❑Once a week take note of the inventory needed to restock merchandise

❑Through out the day take notes of what people buy the most of the inventory purpose

❑Make sure all customers have left the building

❑Lock doors

❑Count cash drawer and take out earnings, leave it ready for the next day

❑Throw all trash

❑Make sure employees all leave together and get to their car safe

Daily Notes

Daily Steps

- ❏ Arrive 1 hour prior opening
- ❏ Deactivate alarm
- ❏ Make sure other employees arrive with you
- ❏ Turn on the lights on
- ❏ Make sure air conditioning/heating turned on
- ❏ Make sure merchandise is in order and dusted
- ❏ Check all money in cash register
- ❏ Open doors
- ❏ Have your best customer service attitude
- ❏ Make sure all employees have what they need for their duties
- ❏ Ask customers if they need help in anything
- ❏ Once a week take note of the inventory needed to restock merchandise
- ❏ Through out the day take notes of what people buy the most of the inventory purpose
- ❏ Make sure all customers have left the building
- ❏ Lock doors
- ❏ Count cash drawer and take out earnings, leave it ready for the next day
- ❏ Throw all trash
- ❏ Make sure employees all leave together and get to their car safe

Daily Notes

Daily Steps

- ❏ Arrive 1 hour prior opening
- ❏ Deactivate alarm
- ❏ Make sure other employees arrive with you
- ❏ Turn on the lights on
- ❏ Make sure air conditioning/heating turned on
- ❏ Make sure merchandise is in order and dusted
- ❏ Check all money in cash register
- ❏ Open doors
- ❏ Have your best customer service attitude
- ❏ Make sure all employees have what they need for their duties
- ❏ Ask customers if they need help in anything
- ❏ Once a week take note of the inventory needed to restock merchandise
- ❏ Through out the day take notes of what people buy the most of the inventory purpose
- ❏ Make sure all customers have left the building
- ❏ Lock doors
- ❏ Count cash drawer and take out earnings, leave it ready for the next day
- ❏ Throw all trash
- ❏ Make sure employees all leave together and get to their car safe

Daily Notes

Daily Steps

- ❑ Arrive 1 hour prior opening
- ❑ Deactivate alarm
- ❑ Make sure other employees arrive with you
- ❑ Turn on the lights on
- ❑ Make sure air conditioning/heating turned on
- ❑ Make sure merchandise is in order and dusted
- ❑ Check all money in cash register
- ❑ Open doors
- ❑ Have your best customer service attitude
- ❑ Make sure all employees have what they need for their duties
- ❑ Ask customers if they need help in anything
- ❑ Once a week take note of the inventory needed to restock merchandise
- ❑ Through out the day take notes of what people buy the most of the inventory purpose
- ❑ Make sure all customers have left the building
- ❑ Lock doors
- ❑ Count cash drawer and take out earnings, leave it ready for the next day
- ❑ Throw all trash
- ❑ Make sure employees all leave together and get to their car safe

Daily Notes

Daily Steps

- ☐ Arrive 1 hour prior opening
- ☐ Deactivate alarm
- ☐ Make sure other employees arrive with you
- ☐ Turn on the lights on
- ☐ Make sure air conditioning/heating turned on
- ☐ Make sure merchandise is in order and dusted
- ☐ Check all money in cash register
- ☐ Open doors
- ☐ Have your best customer service attitude
- ☐ Make sure all employees have what they need for their duties
- ☐ Ask customers if they need help in anything
- ☐ Once a week take note of the inventory needed to restock merchandise
- ☐ Through out the day take notes of what people buy the most of the inventory purpose
- ☐ Make sure all customers have left the building
- ☐ Lock doors
- ☐ Count cash drawer and take out earnings, leave it ready for the next day
- ☐ Throw all trash
- ☐ Make sure employees all leave together and get to their car safe

Daily Notes

Daily Steps

- ❑ Arrive 1 hour prior opening
- ❑ Deactivate alarm
- ❑ Make sure other employees arrive with you
- ❑ Turn on the lights on
- ❑ Make sure air conditioning/heating turned on
- ❑ Make sure merchandise is in order and dusted
- ❑ Check all money in cash register
- ❑ Open doors
- ❑ Have your best customer service attitude
- ❑ Make sure all employees have what they need for their duties
- ❑ Ask customers if they need help in anything
- ❑ Once a week take note of the inventory needed to restock merchandise
- ❑ Through out the day take notes of what people buy the most of the inventory purpose
- ❑ Make sure all customers have left the building
- ❑ Lock doors
- ❑ Count cash drawer and take out earnings, leave it ready for the next day
- ❑ Throw all trash
- ❑ Make sure employees all leave together and get to their car safe

Daily Notes

Daily Steps

- ❏ Arrive 1 hour prior opening
- ❏ Deactivate alarm
- ❏ Make sure other employees arrive with you
- ❏ Turn on the lights on
- ❏ Make sure air conditioning/heating turned on
- ❏ Make sure merchandise is in order and dusted
- ❏ Check all money in cash register
- ❏ Open doors
- ❏ Have your best customer service attitude
- ❏ Make sure all employees have what they need for their duties
- ❏ Ask customers if they need help in anything
- ❏ Once a week take note of the inventory needed to restock merchandise
- ❏ Through out the day take notes of what people buy the most of the inventory purpose
- ❏ Make sure all customers have left the building
- ❏ Lock doors
- ❏ Count cash drawer and take out earnings, leave it ready for the next day
- ❏ Throw all trash
- ❏ Make sure employees all leave together and get to their car safe

Daily Notes

Daily Steps

- ❑ Arrive 1 hour prior opening
- ❑ Deactivate alarm
- ❑ Make sure other employees arrive with you
- ❑ Turn on the lights on
- ❑ Make sure air conditioning/heating turned on
- ❑ Make sure merchandise is in order and dusted
- ❑ Check all money in cash register
- ❑ Open doors
- ❑ Have your best customer service attitude
- ❑ Make sure all employees have what they need for their duties
- ❑ Ask customers if they need help in anything
- ❑ Once a week take note of the inventory needed to restock merchandise
- ❑ Through out the day take notes of what people buy the most of the inventory purpose
- ❑ Make sure all customers have left the building
- ❑ Lock doors
- ❑ Count cash drawer and take out earnings, leave it ready for the next day
- ❑ Throw all trash
- ❑ Make sure employees all leave together and get to their car safe

Daily Notes

Daily Steps

- ❑ Arrive 1 hour prior opening
- ❑ Deactivate alarm
- ❑ Make sure other employees arrive with you
- ❑ Turn on the lights on
- ❑ Make sure air conditioning/heating turned on
- ❑ Make sure merchandise is in order and dusted
- ❑ Check all money in cash register
- ❑ Open doors
- ❑ Have your best customer service attitude
- ❑ Make sure all employees have what they need for their duties
- ❑ Ask customers if they need help in anything
- ❑ Once a week take note of the inventory needed to restock merchandise
- ❑ Through out the day take notes of what people buy the most of the inventory purpose
- ❑ Make sure all customers have left the building
- ❑ Lock doors
- ❑ Count cash drawer and take out earnings, leave it ready for the next day
- ❑ Throw all trash
- ❑ Make sure employees all leave together and get to their car safe

Daily Notes

Daily Steps

- ❑ Arrive 1 hour prior opening
- ❑ Deactivate alarm
- ❑ Make sure other employees arrive with you
- ❑ Turn on the lights on
- ❑ Make sure air conditioning/heating turned on
- ❑ Make sure merchandise is in order and dusted
- ❑ Check all money in cash register
- ❑ Open doors
- ❑ Have your best customer service attitude
- ❑ Make sure all employees have what they need for their duties
- ❑ Ask customers if they need help in anything
- ❑ Once a week take note of the inventory needed to restock merchandise
- ❑ Through out the day take notes of what people buy the most of the inventory purpose
- ❑ Make sure all customers have left the building
- ❑ Lock doors
- ❑ Count cash drawer and take out earnings, leave it ready for the next day
- ❑ Throw all trash
- ❑ Make sure employees all leave together and get to their car safe

Daily Notes

Daily Steps

- ☐ Arrive 1 hour prior opening
- ☐ Deactivate alarm
- ☐ Make sure other employees arrive with you
- ☐ Turn on the lights on
- ☐ Make sure air conditioning/heating turned on
- ☐ Make sure merchandise is in order and dusted
- ☐ Check all money in cash register
- ☐ Open doors
- ☐ Have your best customer service attitude
- ☐ Make sure all employees have what they need for their duties
- ☐ Ask customers if they need help in anything
- ☐ Once a week take note of the inventory needed to restock merchandise
- ☐ Through out the day take notes of what people buy the most of the inventory purpose
- ☐ Make sure all customers have left the building
- ☐ Lock doors
- ☐ Count cash drawer and take out earnings, leave it ready for the next day
- ☐ Throw all trash
- ☐ Make sure employees all leave together and get to their car safe

Daily Notes

_____

_____

_____

_____

_____

_____

_____

_____

_____

_____

_____

_____

Daily Steps

- ❑Arrive 1 hour prior opening
- ❑Deactivate alarm
- ❑Make sure other employees arrive with you
- ❑Turn on the lights on
- ❑Make sure air conditioning/heating turned on
- ❑Make sure merchandise is in order and dusted
- ❑Check all money in cash register
- ❑Open doors
- ❑Have your best customer service attitude
- ❑Make sure all employees have what they need for their duties
- ❑Ask customers if they need help in anything
- ❑Once a week take note of the inventory needed to restock merchandise
- ❑Through out the day take notes of what people buy the most of the inventory purpose
- ❑Make sure all customers have left the building
- ❑Lock doors
- ❑Count cash drawer and take out earnings, leave it ready for the next day
- ❑Throw all trash
- ❑Make sure employees all leave together and get to their car safe

Daily Notes

Daily Steps

- ❑Arrive 1 hour prior opening
- ❑Deactivate alarm
- ❑Make sure other employees arrive with you
- ❑Turn on the lights on
- ❑Make sure air conditioning/heating turned on
- ❑Make sure merchandise is in order and dusted
- ❑Check all money in cash register
- ❑Open doors
- ❑Have your best customer service attitude
- ❑Make sure all employees have what they need for their duties
- ❑Ask customers if they need help in anything
- ❑Once a week take note of the inventory needed to restock merchandise
- ❑Through out the day take notes of what people buy the most of the inventory purpose
- ❑Make sure all customers have left the building
- ❑Lock doors
- ❑Count cash drawer and take out earnings, leave it ready for the next day
- ❑Throw all trash
- ❑Make sure employees all leave together and get to their car safe

Daily Notes

Daily
Steps

☐ Arrive 1 hour prior opening

☐ Deactivate alarm

☐ Make sure other employees arrive with you

☐ Turn on the lights on

☐ Make sure air conditioning/heating turned on

☐ Make sure merchandise is in order and dusted

☐ Check all money in cash register

☐ Open doors

☐ Have your best customer service attitude

☐ Make sure all employees have what they need for their duties

☐ Ask customers if they need help in anything

☐ Once a week take note of the inventory needed to restock merchandise

☐ Through out the day take notes of what people buy the most of the inventory purpose

☐ Make sure all customers have left the building

☐ Lock doors

☐ Count cash drawer and take out earnings, leave it ready for the next day

☐ Throw all trash

☐ Make sure employees all leave together and get to their car safe

Daily Notes

Daily Steps

- ❑Arrive 1 hour prior opening
- ❑Deactivate alarm
- ❑Make sure other employees arrive with you
- ❑Turn on the lights on
- ❑Make sure air conditioning/heating turned on
- ❑Make sure merchandise is in order and dusted
- ❑Check all money in cash register
- ❑Open doors
- ❑Have your best customer service attitude
- ❑Make sure all employees have what they need for their duties
- ❑Ask customers if they need help in anything
- ❑Once a week take note of the inventory needed to restock merchandise
- ❑Through out the day take notes of what people buy the most of the inventory purpose
- ❑Make sure all customers have left the building
- ❑Lock doors
- ❑Count cash drawer and take out earnings, leave it ready for the next day
- ❑Throw all trash
- ❑Make sure employees all leave together and get to their car safe

Daily Notes

Daily
Steps

- ☐ Arrive 1 hour prior opening
- ☐ Deactivate alarm
- ☐ Make sure other employees arrive with you
- ☐ Turn on the lights on
- ☐ Make sure air conditioning/heating turned on
- ☐ Make sure merchandise is in order and dusted
- ☐ Check all money in cash register
- ☐ Open doors
- ☐ Have your best customer service attitude
- ☐ Make sure all employees have what they need for their duties
- ☐ Ask customers if they need help in anything
- ☐ Once a week take note of the inventory needed to restock merchandise
- ☐ Through out the day take notes of what people buy the most of the inventory purpose
- ☐ Make sure all customers have left the building
- ☐ Lock doors
- ☐ Count cash drawer and take out earnings, leave it ready for the next day
- ☐ Throw all trash
- ☐ Make sure employees all leave together and get to their car safe

Daily Notes

Daily
Steps

- ❏ Arrive 1 hour prior opening
- ❏ Deactivate alarm
- ❏ Make sure other employees arrive with you
- ❏ Turn on the lights on
- ❏ Make sure air conditioning/heating turned on
- ❏ Make sure merchandise is in order and dusted
- ❏ Check all money in cash register
- ❏ Open doors
- ❏ Have your best customer service attitude
- ❏ Make sure all employees have what they need for their duties
- ❏ Ask customers if they need help in anything
- ❏ Once a week take note of the inventory needed to restock merchandise
- ❏ Through out the day take notes of what people buy the most of the inventory purpose
- ❏ Make sure all customers have left the building
- ❏ Lock doors
- ❏ Count cash drawer and take out earnings, leave it ready for the next day
- ❏ Throw all trash
- ❏ Make sure employees all leave together and get to their car safe

Daily Notes

_____

_____

_____

_____

_____

_____

_____

_____

_____

_____

_____

_____

Daily
Steps

☐ Arrive 1 hour prior opening

☐ Deactivate alarm

☐ Make sure other employees arrive with you

☐ Turn on the lights on

☐ Make sure air conditioning/heating turned on

☐ Make sure merchandise is in order and dusted

☐ Check all money in cash register

☐ Open doors

☐ Have your best customer service attitude

☐ Make sure all employees have what they need for their duties

☐ Ask customers if they need help in anything

☐ Once a week take note of the inventory needed to restock merchandise

☐ Through out the day take notes of what people buy the most of the inventory purpose

☐ Make sure all customers have left the building

☐ Lock doors

☐ Count cash drawer and take out earnings, leave it ready for the next day

☐ Throw all trash

☐ Make sure employees all leave together and get to their car safe

Daily Notes

Daily Steps

- ❑ Arrive 1 hour prior opening
- ❑ Deactivate alarm
- ❑ Make sure other employees arrive with you
- ❑ Turn on the lights on
- ❑ Make sure air conditioning/heating turned on
- ❑ Make sure merchandise is in order and dusted
- ❑ Check all money in cash register
- ❑ Open doors
- ❑ Have your best customer service attitude
- ❑ Make sure all employees have what they need for their duties
- ❑ Ask customers if they need help in anything
- ❑ Once a week take note of the inventory needed to restock merchandise
- ❑ Through out the day take notes of what people buy the most of the inventory purpose
- ❑ Make sure all customers have left the building
- ❑ Lock doors
- ❑ Count cash drawer and take out earnings, leave it ready for the next day
- ❑ Throw all trash
- ❑ Make sure employees all leave together and get to their car safe

Daily Notes

Daily Steps

- ❑ Arrive 1 hour prior opening
- ❑ Deactivate alarm
- ❑ Make sure other employees arrive with you
- ❑ Turn on the lights on
- ❑ Make sure air conditioning/heating turned on
- ❑ Make sure merchandise is in order and dusted
- ❑ Check all money in cash register
- ❑ Open doors
- ❑ Have your best customer service attitude
- ❑ Make sure all employees have what they need for their duties
- ❑ Ask customers if they need help in anything
- ❑ Once a week take note of the inventory needed to restock merchandise
- ❑ Through out the day take notes of what people buy the most of the inventory purpose
- ❑ Make sure all customers have left the building
- ❑ Lock doors
- ❑ Count cash drawer and take out earnings, leave it ready for the next day
- ❑ Throw all trash
- ❑ Make sure employees all leave together and get to their car safe

Daily Notes

Daily Steps

- ❑ Arrive 1 hour prior opening
- ❑ Deactivate alarm
- ❑ Make sure other employees arrive with you
- ❑ Turn on the lights on
- ❑ Make sure air conditioning/heating turned on
- ❑ Make sure merchandise is in order and dusted
- ❑ Check all money in cash register
- ❑ Open doors
- ❑ Have your best customer service attitude
- ❑ Make sure all employees have what they need for their duties
- ❑ Ask customers if they need help in anything
- ❑ Once a week take note of the inventory needed to restock merchandise
- ❑ Through out the day take notes of what people buy the most of the inventory purpose
- ❑ Make sure all customers have left the building
- ❑ Lock doors
- ❑ Count cash drawer and take out earnings, leave it ready for the next day
- ❑ Throw all trash
- ❑ Make sure employees all leave together and get to their car safe

Daily Notes

Daily
Steps

- ❑Arrive 1 hour prior opening
- ❑Deactivate alarm
- ❑Make sure other employees arrive with you
- ❑Turn on the lights on
- ❑Make sure air conditioning/heating turned on
- ❑Make sure merchandise is in order and dusted
- ❑Check all money in cash register
- ❑Open doors
- ❑Have your best customer service attitude
- ❑Make sure all employees have what they need for their duties
- ❑Ask customers if they need help in anything
- ❑Once a week take note of the inventory needed to restock merchandise
- ❑Through out the day take notes of what people buy the most of the inventory purpose
- ❑Make sure all customers have left the building
- ❑Lock doors
- ❑Count cash drawer and take out earnings, leave it ready for the next day
- ❑Throw all trash
- ❑Make sure employees all leave together and get to their car safe

Daily Notes

_____

_____

_____

_____

_____

_____

_____

_____

_____

_____

_____

_____

Daily Steps

- Arrive 1 hour prior opening
- Deactivate alarm
- Make sure other employees arrive with you
- Turn on the lights on
- Make sure air conditioning/heating turned on
- Make sure merchandise is in order and dusted
- Check all money in cash register
- Open doors
- Have your best customer service attitude
- Make sure all employees have what they need for their duties
- Ask customers if they need help in anything
- Once a week take note of the inventory needed to restock merchandise
- Through out the day take notes of what people buy the most of the inventory purpose
- Make sure all customers have left the building
- Lock doors
- Count cash drawer and take out earnings, leave it ready for the next day
- Throw all trash
- Make sure employees all leave together and get to their car safe

Daily Notes

Daily
Steps

- ❑Arrive 1 hour prior opening
- ❑Deactivate alarm
- ❑Make sure other employees arrive with you
- ❑Turn on the lights on
- ❑Make sure air conditioning/heating turned on
- ❑Make sure merchandise is in order and dusted
- ❑Check all money in cash register
- ❑Open doors
- ❑Have your best customer service attitude
- ❑Make sure all employees have what they need for their duties
- ❑Ask customers if they need help in anything
- ❑Once a week take note of the inventory needed to restock merchandise
- ❑Through out the day take notes of what people buy the most of the inventory purpose
- ❑Make sure all customers have left the building
- ❑Lock doors
- ❑Count cash drawer and take out earnings, leave it ready for the next day
- ❑Throw all trash
- ❑Make sure employees all leave together and get to their car safe

Daily Notes

Daily Steps

- ☐ Arrive 1 hour prior opening
- ☐ Deactivate alarm
- ☐ Make sure other employees arrive with you
- ☐ Turn on the lights on
- ☐ Make sure air conditioning/heating turned on
- ☐ Make sure merchandise is in order and dusted
- ☐ Check all money in cash register
- ☐ Open doors
- ☐ Have your best customer service attitude
- ☐ Make sure all employees have what they need for their duties
- ☐ Ask customers if they need help in anything
- ☐ Once a week take note of the inventory needed to restock merchandise
- ☐ Through out the day take notes of what people buy the most of the inventory purpose
- ☐ Make sure all customers have left the building
- ☐ Lock doors
- ☐ Count cash drawer and take out earnings, leave it ready for the next day
- ☐ Throw all trash
- ☐ Make sure employees all leave together and get to their car safe

Daily Notes

Daily
Steps

❑Arrive 1 hour prior opening

❑Deactivate alarm

❑Make sure other employees arrive with you

❑Turn on the lights on

❑Make sure air conditioning/heating turned on

❑Make sure merchandise is in order and dusted

❑Check all money in cash register

❑Open doors

❑Have your best customer service attitude

❑Make sure all employees have what they need for their duties

❑Ask customers if they need help in anything

❑Once a week take note of the inventory needed to restock merchandise

❑Through out the day take notes of what people buy the most of the inventory purpose

❑Make sure all customers have left the building

❑Lock doors

❑Count cash drawer and take out earnings, leave it ready for the next day

❑Throw all trash

❑Make sure employees all leave together and get to their car safe

Daily Notes

Daily Steps

- ❑Arrive 1 hour prior opening
- ❑Deactivate alarm
- ❑Make sure other employees arrive with you
- ❑Turn on the lights on
- ❑Make sure air conditioning/heating turned on
- ❑Make sure merchandise is in order and dusted
- ❑Check all money in cash register
- ❑Open doors
- ❑Have your best customer service attitude
- ❑Make sure all employees have what they need for their duties
- ❑Ask customers if they need help in anything
- ❑Once a week take note of the inventory needed to restock merchandise
- ❑Through out the day take notes of what people buy the most of the inventory purpose
- ❑Make sure all customers have left the building
- ❑Lock doors
- ❑Count cash drawer and take out earnings, leave it ready for the next day
- ❑Throw all trash
- ❑Make sure employees all leave together and get to their car safe

Daily Notes

Daily Steps

- ❏ Arrive 1 hour prior opening
- ❏ Deactivate alarm
- ❏ Make sure other employees arrive with you
- ❏ Turn on the lights on
- ❏ Make sure air conditioning/heating turned on
- ❏ Make sure merchandise is in order and dusted
- ❏ Check all money in cash register
- ❏ Open doors
- ❏ Have your best customer service attitude
- ❏ Make sure all employees have what they need for their duties
- ❏ Ask customers if they need help in anything
- ❏ Once a week take note of the inventory needed to restock merchandise
- ❏ Through out the day take notes of what people buy the most of the inventory purpose
- ❏ Make sure all customers have left the building
- ❏ Lock doors
- ❏ Count cash drawer and take out earnings, leave it ready for the next day
- ❏ Throw all trash
- ❏ Make sure employees all leave together and get to their car safe

Daily Notes

Daily Steps

- ☐ Arrive 1 hour prior opening
- ☐ Deactivate alarm
- ☐ Make sure other employees arrive with you
- ☐ Turn on the lights on
- ☐ Make sure air conditioning/heating turned on
- ☐ Make sure merchandise is in order and dusted
- ☐ Check all money in cash register
- ☐ Open doors
- ☐ Have your best customer service attitude
- ☐ Make sure all employees have what they need for their duties
- ☐ Ask customers if they need help in anything
- ☐ Once a week take note of the inventory needed to restock merchandise
- ☐ Through out the day take notes of what people buy the most of the inventory purpose
- ☐ Make sure all customers have left the building
- ☐ Lock doors
- ☐ Count cash drawer and take out earnings, leave it ready for the next day
- ☐ Throw all trash
- ☐ Make sure employees all leave together and get to their car safe

Daily Notes

Daily Steps

- ☐ Arrive 1 hour prior opening
- ☐ Deactivate alarm
- ☐ Make sure other employees arrive with you
- ☐ Turn on the lights on
- ☐ Make sure air conditioning/heating turned on
- ☐ Make sure merchandise is in order and dusted
- ☐ Check all money in cash register
- ☐ Open doors
- ☐ Have your best customer service attitude
- ☐ Make sure all employees have what they need for their duties
- ☐ Ask customers if they need help in anything
- ☐ Once a week take note of the inventory needed to restock merchandise
- ☐ Through out the day take notes of what people buy the most of the inventory purpose
- ☐ Make sure all customers have left the building
- ☐ Lock doors
- ☐ Count cash drawer and take out earnings, leave it ready for the next day
- ☐ Throw all trash
- ☐ Make sure employees all leave together and get to their car safe

Daily Notes

Thank you for buying this book!

If you enjoyed this book, please leave a positive review on Amazon.com

If you didn't enjoy this book, please email me at vhernandez0205@gmail.com and let me know why!